J. WESTON
WALCH
PUBLISHER

# SHAKESPEARE
## MADE EASY

AF730682

# *Henry IV, Part One*

Tanya Grosz & Linda Wendler

# User's Guide
# to
# *Walch Reproducible Books*

Purchasers of this book are granted the right to reproduce all pages.

This permission is limited to a single teacher, for classroom use only.

Any questions regarding this policy or requests to purchase further reproduction rights should be addressed to

Permissions Editor
J. Weston Walch, Publisher
321 Valley Street • P.O. Box 658
Portland, Maine 04104-0658

1 2 3 4 5 6 7 8 9 10

ISBN 0-8251-4611-9



Printed in the United States of America

# Contents

# To the Teacher

As any teacher or student who has read Shakespeare knows, his plays are not easy. They are thought-provoking and complex texts that abound with romance, deceit, tragedy, comedy, revenge, and humanity shown at its very worst as well as its very best. In short, to read Shakespeare is to explore the depths and heights of humanity.

The *Shakespeare Made Easy* Activity Guides are designed by teachers for teachers to help students navigate this journey. Each guide is broken into six sections of four activities and one review. At the end of each guide is a final test, a variety of culminating activities, and an answer key. The activities are meant to aid textual comprehension, provide creative opportunities for the reader to make personal connections with the text, and help busy teachers gain quick access to classroom-tested and age-appropriate activities that make the teaching of Shakespeare an easier task.

Each regular activity, as well as each culminating activity, can be modified to be an individual or a group task, and the reviews and test can be used as quick comprehension checks or formally scored assessments. The guides may be used in conjunction with the Barron's *Shakespeare Made Easy* texts or alone. Ultimately, the *Shakespeare Made Easy* Activity Guides are intended to assist teachers and students in gaining an increased understanding of and appreciation for the reading of Shakespeare.

# Introduction to the Play

## Background to *Henry IV, Part One*

*Henry IV, Part One* is actually a sequel to Shakespeare's play *Richard II.* Richard II was crowned King of England on July 16, 1377, when he was only ten years old. A Regency Council was formed to govern because Richard was so young. The council included six earls, three of which were Richard's uncles: John of Gaunt, the Duke of Lancaster (father of Henry Bolingbroke, who becomes Henry IV); Edmund of Langley (also known as the Duke of York); and Thomas of Woodstock (also known as the Earl of Gloucester).

However, once Richard II became older, he rejected the control of the council and conspired to eliminate their control over England. Also, Richard II alienated many of the old and titled earls of England by lavishing gifts and titles on his favorites, Robert de Vere, Earl of Oxford, and Michael de la Pole, Earl of Suffolk. This led to accusations of treason and great disorder in England. In one of his political moves, Richard II exiled John of Gaunt's son, Henry Bolingbroke, for ten years. Once Henry was out of the picture and John of Gaunt died, Richard changed the exile from ten years to life and took over the estate of Henry's uncle, John of Gaunt. This was an illegal seizure of property and money, and it served to alienate many against Richard II.

Being informed of Richard II's actions regarding his inheritance, Henry Bolingbroke, supported by allies, returned to England to demand his rights to his father's estate. The families who helped Henry in his quest were the earls of Northumberland and Worcester, who were brothers, and Northumberland's son, Hotspur. Not only did Bolingbroke win back his family's estate, but he and his allies also deposed Richard II, imprisoned him, and crowned Henry King Henry IV. One of Henry IV's first acts was to arrange for the murder of the deposed Richard.

The opening of *Henry IV, Part One* continues the story of Henry IV's reign and the problems he faces with his guilt over Richard's death, his struggles with his profligate son Hal, and the growing disloyalty of the earls who helped him achieve the throne.

## Synopsis of *Henry IV, Part One*

### Act one, Scene 1

King Henry IV is disappointed that he cannot launch a crusade to the Holy Land because of all the problems in England. He promises to Westmoreland that he will try to solve England's internal problems. New trouble appears as Westmoreland reports that Glendower, a Welsh chieftan, has captured the King's cousin, Mortimer, and that Mortimer has married the daughter of Glendower. However, King Henry is cheered by the additional report that Hotspur has been successful against the Earl of Douglas and has taken prisoners in the northern part of England near Scotland. While King Henry is pleased with

Hotspur's victory, he is ashamed that his son, Prince Hal, is not more like Hotspur.

**Act one, Scene 2**

In Prince Hal's bachelor pad, Falstaff and Prince Hal josh each other wittily about their drinking. Falstaff, in a teasing way, tries to get Prince Hal to promise that he will not punish Falstaff for his thieving once Hal is King. They are soon joined by Ned Poins, who invites them to a highway robbery, and Falstaff and Prince Hal agree to join the venture. Falstaff leaves, and Poins shares with Prince Hal a way to play a prank on Falstaff. The other men will actually do the robbery, and then Hal and Poins will attack Falstaff's crew and take the money from them. The joke will be enjoying the lies that Falstaff will tell about how the money was "stolen" from him.

Prince Hal remains behind when Poins leaves and speaks a famous soliloquy that tells the audience that Prince Hal knows he will not lead his wanton lifestyle much longer but will soon become a reformed Prince, taking on his proper role of leadership.

**Act one, Scene 3**

At the Court, the King is joined by Worcester, Northumberland, and Hotspur. The King is upset because Hotspur will not turn over the prisoners he captured in Scotland. Hotspur explains why he was unable to release his prisoners, showing his intelligence and high spirits as he berates the "dandy" court messenger who came to him in Scotland. However, King Henry is upset because, long after the encounter with the messenger, Hotspur still holds onto his prisoners, which is an insult to the King. The King is also very concerned because Mortimer seems to have deliberately "lost" to Glendower, showing that Mortimer was not loyal to the King. In fact, Mortimer had been named by Richard II to be the true successor to the throne, not Henry.

The King leaves, threatening Hotspur with punishment if he will not turn over the prisoners and forbidding Hotspur to speak of Mortimer. Hotspur then speaks with his father, Northumberland, and Worcester and says he will holler "Mortimer" into the King's ear and keep all his prisoners. He becomes very agitated thinking of all he did to help the King gain the throne, and now he is being treated in this disrespectful way. From this conversation, we discover that the nobles are very dissatisfied by Henry's treatment of them, and that they have become rebellious. Hotspur's father and Worcester tell him to focus on what to do next. They plan to align with Douglas of Scotland and the Archbishop of York. Then they can unite with Glendower of Wales to defeat the King from both the north and the west.

**Act two, Scene 1**

At an inn yard, two carriers are disgusted by the horrible fleas in the inn and the poor feed given to the horses. They ask the Ostler to bring their horses. Gadshill arrives and asks for the Chamberlain. The Chamberlain, acting as an informer, tells Gadshill that a rich landowner will be traveling nearby. Gadshill promises the Chamberlain a reward for the information.

### Act two, Scene 2

Along a highway near a hill, Prince Hal, Poins, Peto, and Bardoph have hidden Falstaff's horse, realizing how difficult it will be for Falstaff to walk up the hill. They all make jokes about Falstaff's weight. Gadshill enters and tells everyone that the travelers are in a good position to be robbed because they have money that is on its way to the King's bank. Falstaff leads the attack while Hal and Poins remain behind. Falstaff and his men successfully rob the travelers and then begin to share the money they have stolen. Prince Hal and Poins enter, disguised, and steal the money from Falstaff with hardly any blows given from either side.

### Act two, Scene 3

Hotspur has received a letter warning him that his rebellious plan against King Henry IV is flawed and could lead to grave danger. Rather than taking the advice seriously, Hotspur denies all the claims in the letter with great gusto. Hotspur's wife, Kate, asks him why he has been so absent from her life. She insists that Hotspur tell her what is going on, or she will break his little finger. Hotspur refuses to tell her in order to keep his actions a secret. He declares his love for her, however, and tells her that even though he must leave on his secret mission, she can follow after him the next day.

### Act two, Scene 4

At a tavern, Prince Hal asks Ned Poins to help him make fun of a waiter named Francis. Prince Hal is amazed that Francis can fill his life with only serving and saying "Anon." Poins goes into another room and calls for Francis while Prince Hal tries to engage Francis in conversation. The largest part of the conversation is Francis saying "Anon" to Poins while trying to be polite to Prince Hal. Prince Hal then compares the limited life of Francis to the limited life of Hotspur, who only cares about battles and killing.

Falstaff enters the tavern and tells how he was attacked by a hundred men, but he keeps changing his story. The Prince then tells Falstaff that it was he and Poins who robbed him. Falstaff replies that he knew it was Prince Hal by instinct and did not want to harm the heir to the throne. Falstaff says he is glad that he is a coward on instinct.

The Hostess enters and announces that a messenger from the King wishes to speak with Prince Hal. Falstaff reports that the messenger has come to bring Hal back to court because of the rebellion. To prepare Prince Hal for answering his father's charges of irresponsibility, Falstaff and Prince Hal role-play the meeting between Prince Hal and the King.

In the role play, Falstaff tries to encourage Prince Hal to keep Falstaff for a friend and not banish him when Hal is king. Prince Hal, however, gives an answer that can be taken both ways with "I do, I will." A sheriff enters with men to search the inn for the money that was robbed. Falstaff hides behind a tapestry and falls asleep. When the sheriff and his men leave, Prince Hal searches Falstaff's pockets and discovers that he has spent almost all his money on drink and hardly any money on real food. He then tells Peto that the King's money will be returned with interest, and that he will put Falstaff in charge of a small group of foot soldiers.

**Act three, Scene 1**

At Glendower's home, the rebels meet to discuss how to split up the rule of England once they are successful in battle. According to their map, Hotspur will have Scotland, Glendower will have Wales, and Mortimer will have England. During the discussion, Hotspur is impatient with Glendower's claims of spiritual powers and also with his share of the island. Lady Percy and Lady Mortimer come in to say good-bye to their husbands Hotspur and Mortimer. Lady Mortimer sings to her husband in Welsh, and Lady Percy and Hotspur continue their good-natured teasing.

**Act three, Scene 2**

Prince Hal and King Henry meet and discuss Prince Hal's behavior and the troubles in England. King Henry tells Hal not to be like Richard II, a "skipping" King who "ambled," not taking his rule seriously. Prince Hal states that he will now act as he should to support the King and, with his victories over the rebels, will gain more honor than Hotspur.

**Act three, Scene 3**

At the Tavern in Eastcheap, Falstaff and Bardolf joke about Falstaff's becoming thin. The hostess, Madam Quickly, enters, and Falstaff claims that he was robbed while he slept at the inn. The hostess does not believe Falstaff, and states that he is claiming he was robbed to get out of paying his debts to her.

Prince Hal enters and tells the story about how he was the one who picked Falstaff's pocket, but that all that was in the pocket was bills and one piece of candy. Then he says he has taken the stolen money to the King's bank where it belongs. Falstaff is sad that the money is gone. Prince Hal tells Falstaff that he must command some foot soldiers because the rebellion is growing against the King. Then Prince Hal departs to command his army.

**Act four, Scene 1**

Hotspur, Worcester, and Douglas are readying for battle in the rebel camp near Shrewsbury. A messenger arrives to announce that Hotspur's father, Northumberland, is ill and cannot come to the battle. The rebels realize that this will be very harmful to their cause. Then Vernon arrives to announce that King Henry IV is coming with a huge army of thirty thousand troops, and that Prince Hal is a leader, wearing his battle armor with glory. He further tells them that Glendower is unable to bring together his army to support the rebels. Hotspur, however, is undeterred from the fight and is willing to die for the rebel cause.

**Act four, Scene 2**

Falstaff has assembled an army of ragtag men—former prisoners, those out on their luck, and other unsavory types. He has earned illegal money by drafting young men about to be married or who are wealthy, and these men pay a bribe to Falstaff in order to be relieved of military duty. Prince Hal arrives and is unhappy about Falstaff's army, but orders his troops to the field of battle at Shrewsbury. Falstaff is not at all eager to fight.

**Act four, Scene 3**

In the rebel camp, Vernon, Worcester, Hotspur, and Douglas debate about the best time to begin the battle. Hotspur wants to attack right away, but Vernon thinks that waiting is better.

They receive an ambassador from King Henry. Sir Walter Blunt enters and asks them to state their case. He says the King will try to make things right. Hotspur tells about how Henry originally wanted only to regain his inheritance and that overthrowing Richard II was wrong, and since becoming King, Henry has insulted Hotspur and committed "wrong on wrong." Blunt asks if this is the message he should bring to King Henry. Hotspur replies that he will think about the offer from the King during the night.

**Act four, Scene 4**

Realizing that Hotspur and the rebels have a slim chance of victory over the forces of the King, the Archbishop of York takes steps to protect himself. He sends letters to his friends to prepare against retaliation from the King.

**Act five, Scene 1**

Worcester and Vernon enter the King's camp. The King expresses his wish that there not be a fight, but that they settle their problems peacefully. Worcester is unwilling to settle, saying that the King has usurped the throne from Richard II. The King is unhappy about their views, but says he is willing to pardon the rebels if they will turn away from the battle. He instructs them to give to Hotspur this message of peace.

Falstaff, in a soliloquy, offers his opinion about honor, which is that it is not helpful to someone who has died.

**Act five, Scene 2**

Worcester and Vernon decide not to inform Hotspur of the King's offer of peace. They are afraid that they will be targets even if the King promises amnesty. Worcester and Vernon discuss how Prince Hal offered high respect for Hotspur. Hotspur and the rebels prepare for battle by Hotspur calling out the battle cry of the Percy family, "Esperance."

**Act five, Scene 3**

Blunt and Douglas fight each other on the battlefield. Blunt has been trying to confuse the enemy by dressing as King Henry IV. Thinking that Blunt is the King, Douglas slays him. Hotspur arrives and informs Douglas that he has killed the noble Blunt, not King Henry. They leave to continue the battle.

Hal finds Falstaff and asks him to keep fighting. He asks Falstaff for his sword; instead, Falstaff offers him his pistol in its case. However, when Hal opens the case, it holds not a pistol but a bottle of sack—cheap alcohol. Prince Hal leaves in disgust.

### Act five, Scene 4

At another part of the battlefield, Prince Hal, his brother John of Lancaster, Westmoreland, and the King gather to rest and assess their position. Prince Hal has received a wound, but he does not let his injury stop him from fighting.

Douglas arrives and begins to fight the King, unsure if he is the real King or another soldier in disguise. The King is almost overcome by Douglas, but Prince Hal arrives and rescues his father, and Douglas flees away. King Henry now realizes the valor and loyalty of his son. The King goes to another part of the battle, and Hal stays on the scene.

Hotspur enters and begins to fight with Prince Hal. Falstaff enters and cheers on Prince Hal. Then Douglas enters and fights with Falstaff. Falstaff drops down on the ground as if he is dead. Prince Hal kills Hotspur, who is dismayed at his loss of titles and honor more than at his own death.

Prince Hal sees Falstaff on the ground and assumes that Falstaff is dead. He leaves the scene. However, Falstaff gets up and explains in a soliloquy that he only pretended to be dead to save himself from Douglas. Falstaff then sees the body of Hotspur and acts as if he, and not Prince Hal, has killed Hotspur.

Prince Hal and his brother enter and see Falstaff carrying Hotspur's body. Falstaff claims that both he and Hotspur rose up after Prince Hal left, and that he was the one who killed Hotspur. Prince Hal allows Falstaff to keep his false claim. As Falstaff leaves the scene, he promises to mend his ways and reform.

### Act five, Scene 5

Victory trumpets sound for the King. It is now time to deal with the rebels. King Henry commands that Vernon and Worcester be killed because they chose not to tell Hotspur of his wish to settle peaceably. If they had given his message truthfully, many would still be alive who are now dead. However, Douglas is pardoned for his valor. The King then lays plans to attack the Archbishop at York and Glendower in Wales. The King and his supporters are pleased with their victory, but they know that further battles lie ahead.

## Character List for *Henry IV, Part One*

### The King, his family, and his supporters

*King Henry IV:* He gained the throne of England by a military overthrow of Richard II. He also is called Bolingbroke.

*Henry, Prince of Wales:* He is known as Prince Hal or Harry. Son of Henry IV, he is fun-loving and mischievous, more often in the bars than at court.

*John of Lancaster:* Prince Hal's younger brother; he is a good son but does not have the charisma of Prince Hal.

*The Earl of Westmoreland:* A nobleman who assists in King Henry IV's army

*Sir Walter Blunt:* A nobleman who assists in King Henry IV's army

### Rebels against the king

*Henry Percy:* He is called Hotspur. He is fiery spirited but has a strong code of honor. He loves his wife Kate, but loves honor more. At the beginning of the play, Henry IV wishes his son, Prince Hal, were more like the honorable Hotspur.

*Henry Percy, Earl of Northumberland:* Referred to in the play as Northumberland; he is Hotspur's father. He helped in the overthrow of Richard II to place Henry IV on the throne, but now he distrusts Henry IV and wishes to overthrow him.

*Thomas Percy, Earl of Worcester:* Referred to in the play as Worcester; brother to Henry Percy and uncle to Hotspur. At the end of the play, he betrays Hotspur by withholding important information.

*Lady Percy:* Wife to Hotspur; Kate is witty, wise, and affectionate. She is also the sister of Edmund Mortimer, Earl of March.

*Edmund Mortimer, Earl of March:* Referred to in the play as Mortimer; brother to Lady Percy. He has a claim to the throne as a descendent of Richard II and is actually a cousin of Henry IV.

*Owen Glendower:* A great leader from Wales and self-proclaimed magician

*Lady Mortimer:* Married to Mortimer and daughter of Owen Glendower. She speaks only Welsh and her husband, Mortimer, speaks only English.

*Archibald, Earl of Douglas:* Referred to in the play as Douglas. A leader of the Scottish army against Henry IV. He is a hot-tempered but also a noble man, whose worth is ultimately valued by Prince Hal.

*Richard Scroop, Archbishop of York:* An ally of the Percy family in their rebellion against the King

*Sir Michael:* An attendant of the Archbishop of York

*Sir Richard Vernon:* A noblemen in the rebellion. He conspires with Worcester to withhold important information from the King for Hotspur.

### The Boar's Head Tavern crew

*Sir John Falstaff:* The funny, rotund, witty companion of Prince Hal. Unlike Hotspur, Falstaff values life more than honor.

*Ned Poins:* Prince Hal's tavern friend. He plans a joke on Falstaff that maintains the Prince's honor and humor.

*Bardolph:* A drinking companion of Prince Hal. Known for his nose that is very red from too much alcohol consumption.

*Peto:* Another drinking companion of Prince Hal

*Gadshill:* He arranges the highway robbery.

*Francis:* A waiter at the Boar's Head Tavern. He always says, "Anon," which means, "I will help you presently."

*Vintner:* The tavern keeper

*Mistress Quickly:* The jovial hostess of the Boar's Head Tavern

### The Stable Crew

*First Carrier:* Carries goods to customers using a packhorse

*Second Carrier*

*Hostler:* A groomer in a stable

*Chamberlain:* Takes care of rooms in an inn, and sometimes sets up the travelers for robbery

*First Traveler*

### Other Minor Characters

*Sheriff, Servant to Hotspur, Messenger, Second Messenger, Soldiers, Travelers, Lords, Attendants*

## Shakespeare and Stage Directions

The plays of Shakespeare are so well written that they seem to leap off the page and come to life. However, the plays themselves have very few stage directions. Perhaps this is because Shakespeare's plays were performed in large amphitheaters that were very simple.

This was a time before electric lights, so the plays needed to take place during the day to utilize the natural light. The average time for a performance was between noon and two in the afternoon. Theater historians report that there were typically no intermissions; plays ran from beginning to end without a break and took about two hours.

The set might be painted canvas to illustrate whether the play was occurring in a forest or a town, for example. Sometimes the background was accompanied by a sign that indicated the place as well. Props were few and large: a table, a chariot, gallows, a bed, or a throne.

However, the audience attending Shakespeare's plays expected a spectacle for the price of admission. Therefore, there were many devices to produce a gasp from the audience. For example, a device in the loft of the theater could raise and lower actors so that they could play gods, ghosts, or other unusual characters. Additionally, a trapdoor in the stage offered a chance for a quick appearance or disappearance. The actors could suggest a beheading or hanging with various illusions on the stage. Sound effects suggesting thunder, horses, or war were common. Music was important, and drums and horns were often played.

Most important to the sense of spectacle were the costumes worn by the actors. These were elaborate, colorful, and very expensive. Therefore, they often purchased these outfits from servants who had inherited the clothes from their masters or from hangmen, who received the clothes of their victims as payment for their services.

Though Shakespeare's stage directions are sparse, definition of a few key terms will be helpful for the reader. The following is a brief glossary of stage directions commonly found in Shakespeare's plays.

### Selected Glossary of Stage Directions in Shakespeare's Plays

**Above:** an indication that the actor speaking from above is on a higher balcony or other scaffold that is higher than the other actors

**Alarum:** a stage signal that calls the soldiers to battle; usually trumpets, drums, and shouts

**Aside:** words spoken by the actor so the audience overhears but the other actors on the stage do not. An aside may also be spoken to one other actor so that the others on stage do not overhear.

**Calls within:** a voice offstage that calls to a character on the stage

**Curtains:** Curtains were fabrics draped around a bed that could be opened or closed for privacy.

**Draw:** Actors pull their swords from their sheaths.

**Enter:** a direction for a character to enter the stage. This can be from the audience's right (stage right) or the audience's left (stage left).

**Enter Chorus:** a direction for an actor to come to the center of the stage and offer some introductory comments, usually in blank verse or rhyming couplets. In *Romeo and Juliet*, the Chorus delivers a sonnet, a form of poetry associated with love.

**Exeunt:** All characters leave the stage, or those characters named leave the stage.

**Exit:** One character leaves the stage.

**Flourish:** A group of trumpets or other horn instruments play a brief melody.

**Have at:** Characters begin to fight, usually with swords.

**Pageant:** a show or spectacle of actors in unusual costumes, usually without words

**Prologue:** an introduction spoken by the Chorus that gives an overview to the audience and invites them into the play or scene

**Retires:** A character slips away.

**Sennet:** a series of notes sounded on brass instruments to announce the approach or departure of a procession

**Singing:** a signal for the actor to sing the following lines as a tune

**Within:** voices or sounds occurring offstage but heard by the audience

# *Introduction to Shakespeare*

## A Brief Biography of William Shakespeare

William Shakespeare was born in April 1564 to John and Mary Shakespeare in Stratford-upon-Avon, England. His birthday is celebrated on April 23. This is memorable because April 23 is also the day Shakespeare died in 1616.

Shakespeare was the eldest of nine children in his family, six of whom survived to adulthood.

William Shakespeare's father worked with leather and became a successful merchant early in his career. He held some relatively important government offices. However, when William was in his early teens, his father's financial position began to slide due to growing debt. After many years, John Shakespeare's fortunes and respect were restored, but records indicate that the years of debt and lawsuits were very stressful.

Historians assume that young Will went to school and took a rigorous course of study including Latin, history, and biblical study. In 1582, at the age of eighteen, he married Anne Hathaway, who was three months pregnant. Studies of Elizabethan family life indicate that Anne's situation was not unusual since it was accepted that the engagement period was as legally binding as the marriage. The couple had a daughter, Susanna, followed by twins, Hamnet and Judith. Not much is known about Shakespeare during the next seven years, but his name is listed as an actor in London by 1592. This was a difficult time for the theater because measures to prevent the spread of the plague regularly closed the theaters.

Between 1594 and 1595, Shakespeare joined the Chamberlain's Men as a playwright and an actor. The acting company featured actor Richard Burbage, and they were a favorite of Queen Elizabeth I. During this time, Shakespeare was writing such plays as *Romeo and Juliet* and *A Midsummer Night's Dream.* Even though Shakespeare was enjoying great success by the time he was 32, it was dampened by the death of his son, Hamnet, in 1596. Soon after, Shakespeare refocused on his home in Stratford where he bought an estate called New Place, with gardens, orchards, and barns in addition to the main home. He still maintained a home in London near the theater.

In 1599, Shakespeare wrote *Henry V*, *Julius Caesar*, and *As You Like It.* The Globe Playhouse was up and running, with Shakespeare a 10 percent owner. This means that he was able to earn 10 percent of any show's profits. This business position helped him solidify his wealth.

In 1603, Shakespeare's reputation earned his acting troop the sponsorship of James I, who requested one play performance per month. Their name changed to the King's Men. By this time, Shakespeare had written and performed in almost all of his comedies and histories. He was proclaimed the finest playwright in London.

But Shakespeare still had what is considered his finest writing to do. He began his writing of tragedies beginning with *Hamlet* in 1600. In the following five years, Shakespeare wrote *Macbeth, Othello,* and *King Lear.* Why Shakespeare turned to these darker, more serious themes is widely debated by scholars. But all agree that these plays established Shakespeare's premier place in English literature.

Toward the end of 1609 through 1610, Shakespeare began to write his problem romances. These works, *The Winter's Tale, Cymbeline,* and *The Tempest,* are rich with mature themes of forgiveness, grace, and redemption.

After 1611, at the age of 47, Shakespeare moved back to Stratford exclusively, settling into life at New Place and enjoying a renewed relationship with his daughters, especially Susanna. He prepared a will, which has become famous for the request to leave his wife their "second best bed." Many have debated whether this is a sentimental or cynical bequest. In the same year that his daughter Judith married, 1616, Shakespeare died at the age of 52. However, it was not until 1623 that all his plays were collected into one manuscript, now referred to as the *First Folio.* The fellow King's Men players who compiled the manuscript, Heming and Condell, entitled it *Mr. William Shakespeare's Comedies, Histories, and Tragedies.*

## Shakespeare's England

The age of Shakespeare was a glorious time for England. William Shakespeare's life in England was defined by the reign of Queen Elizabeth I (1558–1603). During her leadership, England became an important naval and economic force in Europe and beyond.

England's rise to power came when its navy defeated the Spanish Armada in 1588, when Shakespeare was about 24 years old. Queen Elizabeth was skillful in navigating through the conflicts of religion. She maintained religious independence from Rome as the Church of England became firmly rooted during her reign. Additionally, she financed the establishment of colonies in America to grow the British Empire and expand its economic opportunities. At the end of her reign, England was the leader in trade, naval power, and culture.

Because of its role as the main economic, political, and cultural center of England, London became the hub of England's prosperity and fame. If anyone wanted to become famous as a poet or dramatic writer during Shakespeare's time, he would need to be in London. In fact, London was full of great writers besides Shakespeare, such as Marlowe, Sidney, and Jonson. Yet, even as London was full of parties, trade, and amusement, it was also full of poverty, crime, and disease. Crime was a large problem, and the main jail in London was called the Clink. Disease and poor sanitation were common. In fact, twice in Shakespeare's lifetime, London endured an outbreak of the plague, which killed thousands upon thousands of people.

Before Queen Elizabeth took the throne, London was a modestly sized city of about 60,000 people. By the time James I took the throne at her death, more than 200,000 people lived in London and its suburbs. People were attracted to London because it gave many opportunities for work and financial improvement. It was also a vibrant social scene for the upper class. In fact, one honor of being a noble was the opportunity to house Queen Elizabeth and her entire party if she was in your neighborhood. If she were a guest, it was expected that her noble hosts would cover all the expenses of housing her group. She made many "progresses" through England and London, establishing her relationships with the nobility. However, several nobles asked to be released from this honor because the expense of supporting her visit had often caused them bankruptcy.

Perhaps it was better to be a flourishing member of the English merchant middle class. Their numbers and influence were rising in England at the time of Shakespeare. This was a new and an exciting development in Western European history. One major factor in the rise of the middle class was the need for wool for clothing. The expansion of the wool trade led to the formation of entire cities throughout England and sparked progress in many other areas of commerce and trade.

With the rise of the middle class came a concern for more comfortable housing. Rather than serving simply as shelter or defense against attack, housing developed architecturally and functionally. One major improvement was the use of windows to let in light. Also, houses were built with lofts and special places for eating and sleeping, rather than having one multifunctional room. However, doors between rooms were still very rare, so that privacy in Shakespeare's time did not really exist.

Meals in Shakespeare's England were an important part of the day. Breakfast was served before dawn and was usually bread and a beverage. Therefore, everyone was really hungry for the midday meal, which could last up to three hours. If meat was available in the home, it was usually served at this time. A smaller supper was eaten at 6:00 or 7:00 P.M., with the more wealthy people able to eat earlier and the working class eating later. Cooking was dangerous and difficult since all meals were cooked over an open fire. Even bread was not baked in an oven but was cooked in special pans placed over the fire. A pot was almost always cooking on the fire, and the cook would put in whatever was available for supper. This is most likely where the term "potluck" came from.

Furniture was usually made of carved wood, as woodcarving was a developing craft in Shakespeare's day. One important part of an Elizabethan home was the table, or "board." One side was finished to a nice sheen, while the other side was rough. Meals were served on the rough side of the board, and then it was flipped for a more elegant look in the room. The table is where we get the terms "room and board" and having "the tables turned." Another important part of a middle or an upper-class home was the bed. Rather than being made of prickly straw, mattresses were now stuffed with softer feathers. Surrounded by artistically carved four posts, these beds were considered so valuable that they were often a specifically named item in a will.

Clothing in Shakespeare's time was very expensive. Of course, servants and other lower-class people wore simple garb, often a basic blue. But if a person wanted to display his wealth, his clothing was elaborate and colorful, sewn with rich velvet, lace, and gold braid. An average worker might earn seven or eight English pounds in a year, and a very nice outfit for a nobleman might cost as much as 50 or 60 pounds. In other words, if seven or eight healthy workers pooled their money for the entire year, spending nothing else, they could buy only one respectable nobleman's outfit.

Entertainment was an important part of life in Shakespeare's England. Popular sports were bear-baiting, cockfighting, and an early form of bowling. Bear-baiting, in which a dog was set loose to fight with up to three chained bears in the center of an amphitheater, and cockfighting, in which roosters pecked each other to death, were popular then but would be absolutely unacceptable entertainment today. Bowling, however, has maintained its popularity in our current culture.

In London, a main source of entertainment was the theater. Some theaters were very large and could hold more than two thousand people. Even poor people could attend the theater since entrance cost only one penny (equivalent to 60 cents today), and they could stand around the stage. For a bit more money, a person could sit in an actual seat during the performance. However, some thought that going to the theater could be dangerous to your body or your soul. The theaters were closed twice during the plagues to reduce the spread of the disease. The Puritans disapproved of the theater as an unwholesome leisure time activity. And the Puritans also disliked the theater because the theaters were located in an area of London surrounded by brothels and bars. Nevertheless, the theater became respectable enough by 1603 to be supported by James I—and he was the monarch who directed the King James Version of the Bible to be translated.

ACTIVITY 1

# *Clarifying Circumstances*

**Act one, Scenes 1–3**

**Background** *Henry IV, Part One* can be a confusing play due to the many characters and events.

**Directions** Find the answers to the following questions so that you have a clearer picture of who are allies or enemies and what is occurring as the play begins. Use another sheet of paper, if necessary.

1. Based on the King's opening speech, what is a crusade (the battle that the king talks about when he says that all men shall join and "march one way")? Who are they fighting and for what purpose?

2. Why does King Henry have to put off the crusade?

3. Who was captured by the Welsh bandit Glendower?

4. The King's son, Henry, Prince of Wales, is also referred to as ___________ by his father and ___________ by Falstaff.

5. Henry (also referred to as Harry) Percy, commonly known as Hotspur, fought against whom and won? Who were his prisoners?

6. Concerning his son (the Prince) and Hotspur, what does the King wish? How do the two young men compare in the King's eyes (refer to Scene 1, lines 77–90)?

7. According to Westmoreland, why is Hotspur not relinquishing all of his prisoners to the King?

*(continued)*

ACTIVITY 1

# *Clarifying Circumstances* (continued)

8. How do the Prince, Falstaff, and friends make their living (refer to Scene 2)?

9. Does the Prince ever plan to reform his "wicked" ways? How do you know?

10. How does Hotspur explain his not giving the King his prisoners?

11. Hotspur wants his brother-in-law, Mortimer, ransomed from Glendower, who is holding Mortimer captive. Why is the King (for whom Mortimer was fighting) angry with Mortimer, and why does he refuse to pay the ransom (refer to Scene 3, lines 76–91)?

12. Hotspur defends Mortimer to the King in Scene 3, lines 91–111. Write his response in your own words.

13. According to Hotspur, Worcester, and Northumberland, why does the King *really* dislike Mortimer?

14. What part did Worcester and Northumberland play in the previous king's (Richard II's) death?

ACTIVITY 2

# *Paraphrasing the Prince*

**Act one, Scene 2**

**Background** The prince and his friends spend most of this scene carousing in his apartment. After they leave, Prince Henry delivers a soliloquy during which we learn that he does not plan to lead his present lifestyle much longer.

**Directions** Write the speech by Prince Henry in lines 181–203 in your own words to better understand why he seems to embrace the criminal lifestyle despite his royalty.

ACTIVITY 3

# *Falstaff the Clown*

**Act one, Scene 2**

**Background** John Falstaff is one of the most beloved comic foils in all of Shakespeare's plays. He was hugely popular with Elizabethan audiences. Shakespeare wrote him into one of his comedies, *The Merry Wives of Windsor.*

**Directions** Read the following "facts" about John Falstaff, and then find the line(s) in Act one, Scene 2 that support(s) or demonstrate(s) it.

| **Fact** | **Line(s) of Support** |
|---|---|
| ✓ Falstaff is a drunk. | |
| ✓ Falstaff likes women. | |
| ✓ Falstaff is not proud about money. | |
| ✓ Falstaff cares for his friend Hal. | |
| ✓ Falstaff steals for a living. | |
| ✓ Falstaff is overweight and gluttonous. | |
| ✓ Falstaff tells tall tales about his achievements. | |

ACTIVITY 4

# *The King's Spy*

**Act one, Scene 3**

**Background** In Act one, Scene 3, Hotspur, Northumberland, and Worcester begin to plot a rebellion against King Henry IV.

**Directions** Imagine that you are one of King Henry's most trusted spies. Compose a brief report ($\frac{1}{2}$ to $\frac{3}{4}$ of a page) in which you detail the treasonous words shared between Hotspur, Northumberland, and Worcester in lines 180–296.

 

ACTIVITY 5

# *Review*

**Directions** Answer the following. Write the letter of the correct answer in the space provided.

___ 1. This play takes place in what country?
- a. Scotland
- b. Norway
- c. England
- d. Denmark

___ 2. Which event(s) make the King put off his crusade?
- a. The Welsh bandit Glendower captured Mortimer.
- b. His own people are staging a rebellion against him.
- c. Hotspur won't give up all of his prisoners to the King.
- d. Both a and c

___ 3. What kind of practical joke has Poins planned for Falstaff and the other thieves?
- a. Prince Harry will pretend to arrest all of them for pickpocketing.
- b. Poins and the Prince will rob the thieves.
- c. Poins has dug a sinkhole into which the thieves will fall as they try to rob people.
- d. None of the above

___ 4. Another name for Harry Percy is:
- a. the Prince
- b. Worcester
- c. Hal
- d. Hotspur

___ 5. How does Hotspur explain his refusal to give the King his prisoners?
- a. He did not really refuse, but the messenger's haughty air made him angry and he replied curtly.
- b. He has no intention of releasing the prisoners until Mortimer is ransomed.
- c. There are no prisoners; Hotspur has executed them all.
- d. The messenger misunderstood, and Hotspur will gladly give the King all of the prisoners.

___ 6. What does Hotspur believe is the true reason for the King's disdain of Mortimer?
- a. Mortimer was named by King Richard II as the next heir to the throne.
- b. Mortimer is treasonous.
- c. The King is in love with Mortimer's wife.
- d. The King is afraid of Glendower.

___ 7. Hotspur is holding prisoners from what country?
- a. England
- b. Scotland
- c. Norway
- d. France

*(continued)*

 

# *Review (continued)*

___ 8. Who is Hotspur's father?

a. Worcester
b. Northumberland
c. Mortimer
d. King Henry

___ 9. Which armies will join the rebels in opposing the King?

a. Scottish and Yorkist
b. Norwegian and Belgian
c. French and Scottish
d. Finnish and English

___ 10. How does the King feel about his own son?

a. He wishes he were more like Hotspur.
b. He thinks his son will make a fine leader one day.
c. He is angry at his son for not being at the meeting.
d. None of the above

ACTIVITY 6

# *Kingly Concern*

**Act two, Scenes 1 and 2**

**Background** As we learned earlier, the King is alternatively frustrated with or worried about his son, Prince Hal.

**Directions** Imagine that you are one of the King's most loyal servants sent to spy on Hal to discover what he is up to and what kind of people he consorts with. Describe everything that has occurred involving the Prince up through Act two, Scene 2, including descriptions of the people he surrounds himself with (Falstaff, Poins, and so forth). Suggested length: 1 page to $1\frac{1}{2}$ pages. You will need to use another sheet of paper for this activity.

ACTIVITY 7

# *Falstaff*



**Background** John Falstaff is a most memorable character. He is all about excess—too much wine, too many women, too much food, too much thieving, too much exaggeration. However, besides this excess, we know relatively little about him.

**Directions** Fill in the following prompts by using what you know of Falstaff from the text and by using your imagination. Extra credit: On another sheet of paper, draw a picture of Falstaff as you envision him!

Middle name:

Parents' names and occupations:

Girlfriend? Ever been married?

Favorite meal:

Greatest fear:

Children?

Greatest indulgence:

Favorite drink:

Attitude toward royalty:

Attitude toward the poor:

Favorite saying:

Hidden talent:

Greatest ambition:

ACTIVITY 8

# *Lady Percy Responds*

**Act two, Scene 3**

**Background** In this scene, Lady Percy (Kate) tries to get her husband to tell her where he is going, why he has not been eating or sleeping well lately, and what he is planning. He dismisses all of her questions and insults her sex (see lines 97–109).

**Directions** Imagine that you are Kate. Respond to all Hotspur said or did not say in a letter revealing your hurt and frustration with his brusque manner. Suggested length: 1 page. Use another sheet of paper, if necessary.

ACTIVITY 9

# *Falstaff's Tall Tales*

**Act two, Scene 4**

**Background** In Act two, Scene 4, Falstaff lies about the "ambush" he and his fellow thieves suffered. It was really the Prince and Poins who robbed them, knowing that Falstaff would later lie about his own courage in the face of danger.

**Directions** Using this scene as a model, invent another tall tale for Falstaff to tell about that robbery. Suggested length: $\frac{3}{4}$ of a page to 1 page. Use another sheet of paper, if necessary.

ACTIVITY 10

# Review

**Directions** Read each statement and decide if it is true or false. Then write true (T) or false (F) in the space provided.

_____ 1. Falstaff thinks that Poins has hidden his horse.

_____ 2. Falstaff knows that Poins and the Prince are the disguised thieves who rob him.

_____ 3. Though Hotspur will not tell his wife where he is going, he will allow her to join him.

_____ 4. The Prince teases the innkeeper for fun.

_____ 5. Falstaff keeps changing the numbers of the men that he claims robbed him.

_____ 6. Bardolph has a very bad complexion.

_____ 7. The Prince lies to the Sheriff about Falstaff's location.

_____ 8. Falstaff is a thin and fragile man.

_____ 9. During Act two, a nobleman from the court comes to tell the Prince that he must go to see his father.

_____ 10. Hal is the Prince of Wales.

_____ 11. The tavern that Falstaff and the Prince stay at is called the Boar's Head Tavern.

_____ 12. Hotspur usurps Henry's throne in this act.

ACTIVITY 11

# *Values Profile: Hotspur vs. Hal*

**Background** The historical Hotspur was much older than the historical Prince Henry, but Shakespeare makes them close to the same age for this play. This encourages audiences to compare their characters and the choices they have made in life.

**Directions** Reread the lines spoken by Hotspur and Prince Hal thus far, and consider what kind of people they are based on what you have read. Then rank the values listed below using 1 for most important, 2 for somewhat important, or 3 for unimportant. Next to each ranking, give a reason or a line from the play to support your ranking.

**Hotspur**

| **Rank** | **Values/Traits** | **Support for Rank** |
|---|---|---|
| _____ | Honesty | |
| _____ | Loyalty | |
| _____ | Ambition | |
| _____ | Material wealth | |
| _____ | Kindness | |
| _____ | Power | |
| _____ | Love | |
| _____ | Duty | |
| _____ | Honor | |
| _____ | Courage | |
| _____ | Morality | |
| _____ | Fun | |

*(continued)*

ACTIVITY 11

# *Values Profile: Hotspur vs. Hal* (continued)

**Prince Hal**

| **Rank** | **Values/Traits** | **Support for Rank** |
|---|---|---|
| _____ | Honesty | |
| _____ | Loyalty | |
| _____ | Ambition | |
| _____ | Material wealth | |
| _____ | Kindness | |
| _____ | Power | |
| _____ | Love | |
| _____ | Duty | |
| _____ | Honor | |
| _____ | Courage | |
| _____ | Morality | |
| _____ | Fun | |

ACTIVITY 12

# *Glendower's Claims*

**Act three, Scene 1**

**Background** Glendower and Hotspur both think very highly of themselves. Hotspur, however, absolutely refuses to listen to Glendower's boasting in this scene.

**Directions** Reread the following lines and paraphrase Glendower's claims and Hotspur's reaction to or mockery of them.

| **Glendower's Lines** | **Hotspur's Lines** |
|---|---|
| Lines 11–15; 33–46<br>Paraphrase: | Lines 16–18; 19–20; 22–32<br>Paraphrase: |
| Line 50<br>Paraphrase: | Lines 51 and 52<br>Paraphrase: |
| Line 53<br>Paraphrase: | Lines 54–58<br>Paraphrase: |
| Lines 116–121<br>Paraphrase: | Lines 122–129<br>Paraphrase: |

ACTIVITY 13

# *Haughty Hotspur*

**Acts one–three**

**Background** Throughout *Henry IV, Part One,* the character of Hotspur is particularly vivid.

**Directions** Reread the following scenes involving Hotspur and then answer the questions to get a clearer picture of Hotspur's character and motivation.

1. Act one, Scene 3: How does Hotspur react to the King's servant when asked for the release of the prisoners?

2. Act one, Scene 3: How does Hotspur react after his meeting with the King? Does he intend to give the King what he wants?

3. Act one, Scene 3: How does Hotspur react to Worcester's plan to rebel against the King with the armies of Scotland and York?

4. Act two, Scene 3: How does he react to his wife's concerns about him?

5. Act three, Scene 1: How does Hotspur react to Mortimer and his wife's reactions to their necessary parting?

6. How would you generally describe or characterize Hotspur?

ACTIVITY 14

# *Lady Percy and Lady Mortimer*

**Act three, Scene 1**

**Background** In this scene, notice how differently Hotspur and Mortimer react to leaving their wives in order to go to war.

**Directions** Think about what kind of women would be attracted to each. Then, write a profile of each woman as best you can.

| Question | Lady Mortimer | Lady Percy |
|---|---|---|
| What does each look like? | | |
| What kind of temperament does each have? | | |
| What kind of relationship does each have with her husband? | | |
| How well would each woman conform to the expectations for a wife in that day (subservient, dependent, knowing her place, and so forth)? | | |

ACTIVITY 15

# *Review*

**Directions** Test your understanding of the characters thus far by matching each character with the correct description of him or her. All letters will be used at least once, and some letters will be used more than once. Write the letter of the correct answer in the space provided.

a. King Henry IV
b. Prince Hal
c. Hotspur
d. Lady Mortimer
e. Worcester
f. Glendower
g. Poins
h. Falstaff
i. Mortimer

_____ 1. Refuses to relinquish all prisoners to the King

_____ 2. Speaks only Welsh

_____ 3. Thinks up the plan to rob Falstaff

_____ 4. Wishes his son was more like Hotspur

_____ 5. Claims that the earth shook when he was born

_____ 6. According to the King, foolishly and willfully betrayed the lives of the men he led to fight

_____ 7. Likes to drink and eat in excess

_____ 8. Tells Hotspur of the plan to unite with the armies of York and Scotland to overthrow King Henry IV

_____ 9. Claims that he will reform his wicked ways and become what people expect him to be

_____ 10. Is considered to be a magician or sorcerer

_____ 11. Claims that a hundred men ambushed him

_____ 12. Is forced to interrupt a crusade to deal with conflict at home

ACTIVITY 16

# *A Disappointed Father*

**Act three, Scene 2**

**Background** The discussion that goes on between the King and his son in this scene is as relevant today as it was when Shakespeare was writing it.

**Directions** Reread this scene, and then imagine a modern-day scenario that parallels what is happening between the King and Harry. Write your encounter in modern English. Use play format if you like. Suggested length: 1 page to 2 pages. You will need additional sheets of paper for this activity.

**Scenario example:** A wealthy father is speaking to his wayward son who stands to inherit the family business. The son of the father's competitor is a well-respected young man who has just graduated from Harvard Business School, and the father wants his son to be more like this young man.

ACTIVITY 17

# *Prince Hal's Reflection*

**Act three, Scene 2**

**Background** In this scene, the Prince makes an important decision to change. His father has clearly expressed his disappointment in him, and the Prince vows to make him proud.

**Directions** Imagine that you are the Prince. Write an entry in your journal in which you express remorse for your actions, determination to make your father proud, and anger toward Hotspur. Include your plans to redeem yourself in the eyes of your father and your country. Suggested length: $\frac{3}{4}$ of a page to 1 page. Use another sheet of paper, if necessary.

ACTIVITY 18

# Character Guide

**Background** There are many characters in *Henry IV, Part One.* They are especially hard to keep track of because they occasionally have similar surnames or are referred to by either their names or their titles.

**Directions** In order to get a clearer understanding of the characters in this play, write a brief description of the following characters, and provide an identifying quotation for the characters whose names have asterisks by them. Use another sheet of paper, if necessary.

*Prince Henry (Hal/Harry):

*King Henry IV:

*Sir John Falstaff:

*Harry Percy (Hotspur):

*Glendower

Worcester:

Mortimer:

Northumberland:

Poins:

Westmoreland:

ACTIVITY 19

# *The Hostess Replies*

**Act three, Scene 3**

**Background** In this scene, Falstaff is trying to get out of paying his tavern bill by lying and saying that someone stole his money. To top that, he calls the hostess of the tavern names and insults a gift she gave him (lines 64–67).

**Directions** Imagine that you are the hostess who has, up to this point, put up with Falstaff's tall tales, drunkenness, and inability to pay his bills on time. These lies and insults are the last straw. Compose a letter in which you tell him that he may *not* stay at your tavern anymore and that if he does not pay you the money he owes you, you will have him put in jail. In this letter, list all of his offenses, including those you discover in this scene and any you make up as fitting with his character and what you know of him so far. Use another sheet of paper, if necessary.

## ACTIVITY 20

# *Review*

**Directions** Read the following quotations from *Henry IV, Part One.* In the space provided, write the letter of the character who spoke the line. Some letters will be used more than once.

a. King b. Prince c. Hotspur d. Falstaff e. Glendower f. Mortimer

_____ 1. "By so much shall I falsify men's hopes; And like bright metal on a sullen ground, my reformation, glitt'ring o'er my fault, shall show more goodly, and attract more eyes than that which hath no foil to set it off."

_____ 2. "But I will lift the down-trod Mortimer as high in the air as this unthankful King, as this ingrate and cankered Bolingbroke."

_____ 3. "Thou hast the most unsavoury similes, and art indeed the most comparative rascalliest sweet young prince."

_____ 4. "Three times hath Henry Bolingbroke made head against my power, thrice from the banks of Wye and sandy-bottomed Severn have I sent him bootless home, and weather-beaten back."

_____ 5. "This is the deadly spite that angers me, my wife can speak no English, I no Welsh."

_____ 6. "I had rather live with cheese and garlic in a windmill, far, than feed on cates and have him talk to me in any summer house in Christendom."

_____ 7. ". . . if I fought not with fifty of them, then I'm a bunch of radish: If there were not two or three and fifty upon poor old Jack, then I am no two-legged creature."

_____ 8. "I do beseech your Majesty may salve the long-grown wounds of my intemperance: If not, the end of life cancels all bands, and I will die a hundred thousand deaths ere break the smallest parcel of this vow."

_____ 9. "It seems then that the tidings of this broil brake off our business for the Holy Land."

_____ 10. "Do not thou when thou art king hang a thief."

 

ACTIVITY 21

# *Bad News for Hotspur*

**Act four, Scene 1**

**Background** In this scene, the news reported to Hotspur goes from bad to worse.

**Directions** Reread the following lines. Then, in your own words, describe the bad news Hotspur receives.

Bad News Item 1, line 16:

Bad News Item 2, lines 31–40:

Bad News Item 3, lines 60–75:

Bad News Item 4, lines 88 and 89:

Bad News Item 5, lines 92–94:

Bad News Item 6, lines 125–127:

ACTIVITY 22

# *Captain Falstaff*

**Act four, Scene 2**

**Background** Falstaff has taken his orders from the Prince and has raised a regiment of soldiers. But he only recruited men who had money to pay Falstaff to accept less experienced and more desperate substitutes.

**Directions** Reread Falstaff's speech about the kinds of soldiers he has recruited. Then, paraphrase his soliloquy in one or two paragraphs. Next, draw a soldier who fits Falstaff's description. Use another sheet of paper, if necessary.

ACTIVITY 23

# Complaints Against the King

**Act four, Scene 3**

**Background** When Sir Walter Blunt asks for grievances against the King, Hotspur has a long and elaborate list to share.

**Directions** Write a list that summarizes, in your own words, Hotspur's accusations against the King. Use bullets, numbers, or letters to organize your list.

ACTIVITY 24

# *The Archbishop's Letter*

**Act four, Scene 4**

**Background** In this scene, we see the Archbishop of York planning a defense of his city against the King's forces in case the King is victorious against Hotspur—an event that looks extremely likely. The Archbishop neatly sums up the situation in his discussion with Sir Michael, his retainer. This scene also sets up events that occur in *Henry IV, Part Two.*

**Directions** After reading the interchange between the Archbishop and Sir Michael, compose a brief letter in which you, as the Archbishop, plead with friends to arm together to oppose the King. Attempt to use Shakespearean language as much as possible, and try to keep your letter and your reasoning behind the pleas true to the dialogue and the events in the text. Suggested length: $^3/_4$ of a page to 1 page. Use another sheet of paper, if necessary.

ACTIVITY 25

# Review

**Directions** Number the following events from the first four acts of *Henry IV, Part One* to match the order in which they occurred.

**Act one**

___ Worcester, Northumberland, and Hotspur plan their rebellion against the King.

___ Poins tells the Prince about his plan to rob Falstaff.

___ Hotspur explains to the King why he has withheld prisoners.

___ The King puts off a crusade to deal with issues at home.

**Act two**

___ Lady Percy questions Hotspur about his behavior.

___ The Prince covers for Falstaff when the local authorities come looking for him.

___ The Prince teases the young waiter Francis.

___ Falstaff runs away from the disguised Prince and Poins.

**Act three**

___ Hotspur antagonizes Glendower when being told of Glendower's birth.

___ Falstaff lies to the hostess of the tavern and says he has been robbed.

___ Hotspur makes fun of the way in which Mortimer and his wife take leave of each other.

___ The Prince vows to his father that he will redeem his name and make him proud.

**Act four**

___ Falstaff contemplates his soldiers.

___ Hotspur is told that his father is too sick to come to battle.

___ The Archbishop and Sir Michael discuss the impending war.

___ Hotspur tells Sir Blunt all of his complaints against the King.

ACTIVITY 26

# *Explanation of the War*

**Act five, Scene 1**

**Background** Before the battle, Worcester declares why the rebels are at war with the King. King Henry responds that his reasons are made simply to entice people to join the rebellion.

**Directions** Based on Worcester's speech in lines 30–70 and Hotspur's complaints against King Henry in Act four, Scene 3, lines 52–88 and 89–106, write a newspaper article that explains the rebels' arguments. Imagine that most of the country will be reading this—you should try to explain causes for defying the King in a way that most common people would understand. Use another sheet of paper, if necessary.

ACTIVITY 27

# *Honor, According to Falstaff*

Act five

**Background** In this act, Falstaff contemplates the concept of honor three times.

**Directions** Reread the passages, and in your own words, summarize what each is saying. Then answer the questions that follow.

**Scene 1, lines 127–140:**

**Scene 3, lines 55–60:**

**Scene 4, lines 110–124:**

## Questions

1. Overall, what does honor mean to Falstaff?

2. How does this definition differ from what you perceive to be Prince Hal's definition of honor?

ACTIVITY 28

# War Correspondent

**Act five**

**Background** In Act five, we see the forces of King Henry and Hotspur clash in battle, and we learn about some tactics of medieval warfare, such as the use of decoys to protect the King.

**Directions** Imagine that you are a war correspondent informing England of how the war is going. Report all that has occurred in Act five, including the King's offer of clemency, who has died, who has won, and so forth. Suggested length: 1–2 pages. You will need additional sheets of paper for this activity.

ACTIVITY 29

# *Headlines for Five Scenes*

**Background** Shakespeare is known for not wasting words in his plays. Generally he jumps right into the action in each scene, with dialogue serving to drive the plot.

**Directions** Choose seven scenes from various acts throughout the play. Keep these in chronological order. Decide which event is central to each of your chosen scenes, and write a headline for each event. Remember that headlines often employ alliteration (**B**rawny **B**adgers **B**ludgeon Eagles in Semifinals), use vivid action verbs, and are straightforward and attention-getting. Generally, articles (a, an, the) are left out of headlines.

Act _____, Scene _____, Headline:

Act _____, Scene _____, Headline:

Act _____, Scene _____, Headline:

Act _____, Scene _____, Headline:

Act _____, Scene _____, Headline:

ACTIVITY 30

# *Review*

**Directions** Read each statement and decide if it is true or false. Then write true (T) or false (F) in the space provided.

_____ 1. Hotspur and Prince Hal argue over who is better fit to rule England.

_____ 2. The King knights Falstaff for his courage on the battlefield.

_____ 3. Glendower claims that the earth shook when he was born.

_____ 4. Hotspur kills the Prince.

_____ 5. The Prince redeems himself through his courage in the midst of war.

_____ 6. Falstaff is killed in battle.

_____ 7. Lady Percy slaps her husband's face after he makes a dirty joke.

_____ 8. Glendower tells Hotspur that if Hotspur crosses him one more time, Glendower will use his powers of darkness against him.

_____ 9. Falstaff role-plays the King for Prince Henry.

_____ 10. England falls into the hands of Scottish resistance fighters.

# Henry IV, Part One

**Final Test**

**Directions:** Read each statement. Then write true (T) or false (F) in the space provided.

___ 1. The last person to die in the play is Hotspur.

___ 2. Lady Mortimer cries when her husband has to leave for the war.

___ 3. Prince Hal kills Hotspur.

___ 4. This play takes place in Scotland.

___ 5. Hotspur is also referred to as Hal.

___ 6. The King sees a ghost.

___ 7. Hotspur is Northumberland's nephew.

___ 8. King Henry refuses to pay Mortimer's ransom.

___ 9. Hotspur is hot-headed.

___ 10. Falstaff is kicked out of the inn/tavern in which he lives.

**Directions:** Choose the letter of the best answer. Write it in the space provided.

___ 11. What is the name of the king King Henry deposed in order to become king?

a. Gadshill
b. Richard
c. Worcester
d. Mortimer

___ 12. Whom did the king prior to King Henry declare heir to the throne?

a. Mortimer
b. Gloucester
c. Worcester
d. Glendower

___ 13. Falstaff says "_________ is a mere scutcheon—and so ends my catechism."

a. Nobility
b. Revenge
c. War
d. Honor

___ 14. Who disguises himself as King Henry on the battlefield?

a. Sir Walter Blunt
b. Harry Percy
c. Westmoreland
d. none of the above

*(continued)*

___ 15. Who kills Hotspur?

a. King Henry
b. Prince Hal
c. Falstaff
d. Sir Walter Blunt

___ 16. The play ends with

a. victory and peace, and everyone returns home to their castles.
b. King Henry sending people off to quell other rebellions.
c. Falstaff and Prince Hal joking around.
d. everyone dying.

___ 17. Who told Hotspur of Prince Hal's challenge to him?

a. Vernon
b. Prince Hal
c. Falstaff
d. Glendower

___ 18. Who is the last person in the play to speak?

a. Prince Hal
b. Hotspur
c. Falstaff
d. King Henry

___ 19. Who decides that Hotspur must not know of King Henry's offer of clemency for the rebels?

a. Worcester
b. Northumberland
c. Vernon
d. Glendower

___ 20. Whom does Falstaff lie about killing in the battle?

a. Hotspur
b. Northumberland
c. Worcester
d. Douglas

CULMINATING ACTIVITY 1

# *Put It to Music*

**Directions** Students should work in groups of no more than four for this activity, and one student in each group must have access to a CD burner. Choose one song to represent each of the five acts in the play. Each song needs to represent the event of central importance to each act. Compile a CD using no more than 30-second splices of each song. After deciding what events are central in importance within each of the acts, type up an explanation of your song choices. Then, present your songs and your reasons. Groups may want to briefly recount the events, or, if they feel the music is obvious enough, they may have the class guess what event each song represents.

## CULMINATING ACTIVITY 2

# *Contemplating King Henry IV*

**Directions** Write a multi-paragraph essay that explores the readers' perception of King Henry IV. Did he misuse and disregard his friends once he attained power, as Worcester and Hotspur claim, or did the King have just cause for his anger with Mortimer and Hotspur? Use events and quotations from the text for support. Suggested length: 3–5 pages. Use the space below to develop an outline of your essay. Then write your essay on additional sheets of paper.

## CULMINATING ACTIVITY 3

# *Create a Movie Poster or a Book Jacket*

**Directions** Imagine that you are the graphic designer for either a movie poster or a book jacket to promote *Henry IV, Part One.* Incorporate one of the major events from the play and as many of the characters as possible into your design. Make the design enticing and colorful, so that anyone seeing it would feel compelled to read the book or see the movie. Make the print and design big and easy to read. Use the space below to sketch out an idea, but use posterboard for the final product.

CULMINATING ACTIVITY 4

# Henry IV, Part One, *the Condensed Version*

**Directions** Take each of the five acts and condense the events and lines into a 3–5-minute version. Write everything in modern-day language, and then stage the 15–20-minute play. The result should be a humorous and concise rendition of the famous play. Write your version below, using additional sheets of paper as needed.

CULMINATING ACTIVITY 5

# *Researching Henry*

**Directions** Though this play is based on real people and events, Shakespeare took liberties with history, rewriting it as he chose. Do some research on Henry IV and Richard II to discover what in this play is true and what has been fictionalized. Then, either write a paper or prepare a presentation that shows what in the play is factual and what is fictional or inaccurate. Use another sheet of paper, if necessary.

CULMINATING ACTIVITY 6

# *The Three-in-One Play*

**Directions** This play encompasses the three genres—history, tragedy, and comedy—in one play. Individually or in small groups, break down the genres within this play and tackle each separately, coming up with a mini-presentation (two minutes per genre) for each genre. Analyze the characters, situations, and events that are prominently featured in each genre, and find lines from the play that support your analysis. For example, in looking at the tragedy within the play, you may focus on Hotspur as a tragic hero. He believes he has been wronged by the King and goes about righting that wrong passionately despite his allies and even his father failing him at the end. He dies more concerned about his loss of glory than his loss of his life. Finally, after you have presented each of the three genres, choose which genre you find to be the most prominent or most compelling in the play and support your choice. The use of visual aids (depictions of characters in the scenes you discuss, a map showing where the action occurs, a graphic organizer of the characters you will discuss, and so forth) is strongly encouraged.

# Henry IV, Part One

**Answer Key**

**Activity 1**

1. The crusade is a battle the king wishes to fight in Jerusalem; Englishmen are fighting to drive non-Christians from the holy lands of Israel.
2. He must put off going to the holy lands because a fellow Englishman and his army were defeated and captured by a Welshman who opposes the king.
3. Mortimer
4. Harry, Hal
5. Hotspur fought against a Scottish army. Some of his prisoners were Mordake, Earl of Fife, and the earls of Athol, Murray, Angus, and Menteith.
6. The King wishes that Hotspur were his son. In the King's eyes, Hotspur is honorable and courageous, and his son just the opposite.
7. He claims that it is his uncle Worcester's doing; he is trying to stir up people against the King.
8. They rob people.
9. Yes; he says so in his long soliloquy in Scene 2 starting on line 181.
10. He was hot and tired after a battle, and the King's messenger arrived all fresh and haughty and patronizing, and it simply made Hotspur angry.
11. The King claims that Mortimer foolishly led his troops into trouble and then reacted with cowardice and surrendered without a real fight.
12. Hotspur says that Mortimer fought valiantly against Glendower for the King.
13. Mortimer was named heir to the throne by the late King Richard II (deposed by King Henry IV).
14. According to Hotspur, they aided and abetted in Richard's murder.

**Activity 2**

Answers will vary, but the following may serve as a guideline:

The prince says that he will go along with Falstaff and his crew's rowdy ways for now, but not always. He compares himself to the sun, who shades itself from the earth so that when it is seen again, everyone is happy and awed by its beauty and warmth. Similarly, he is hiding his courage and splendor right now. He says that his reformation from his wicked ways will seem all the more impressive after his goodness has been hidden, and when he does reform, people will think he was misunderstood and misjudged all along. He claims that he will play this game so well that when he does reform, he will do it better than any black sheep has in history.

**Activity 3**

Answers will vary, but the following may serve as a guideline:

drunk: lines 1–7
women: lines 8, 9
money: lines 50, 53–57
Hal: lines 73 and 74
steals: lines 12, 22–28, 95 and 96, 115–123

overweight: lines 7, 21, 108 and 109, 173
tall tales: lines 169–176

**Activity 4**

Answers will vary, but they should contain the following:

Hotspur claims he will never surrender his prisoners. They discuss the fact that Henry dislikes Mortimer because he was named heir by Richard. Hotspur claims that their reward for helping Henry become king by killing Richard will be their own violent deaths as dictated by Henry. Worcester mentions a dangerous scheme, but Hotspur interrupts and claims that he would consider poisoning the prince. Worcester says that Hotspur should return the Scottish prisoners and get Douglas's son (a Scottish rebel leader) to agree to support them with an army. Then Northumberland will add the Archbishop of York to their list of allies. The armies of Scotland and York will then join with Mortimer and these men (and their armies) to oppose the King. They will all secretly work on forming these alliances, and once they are formed, they will all meet.

**Activity 5**

1. c
2. d
3. b
4. d
5. a
6. a
7. b
8. b
9. a
10. a

**Activity 6**

Answers will vary, but the following may serve as a content guideline:

The prince spends much of his time with John Falstaff, an overweight, drunken thief. They spend much of their time thieving, talking nonsense, or drinking in a tavern. They robbed a wealthy farmer, but Harry and a man named Poins (another thief) wore disguises and robbed their friends for sport. Bardolph, Peto, and Gadshill are other thieves who joined in the robbery only to be robbed by Poins and Harry. His actions and demeanor are a disgrace to the crown.

**Activity 7**

Answers will vary.

**Activity 8**

Answers will vary.

**Activity 9**

Answers will vary.

**Activity 10**

1. T
2. F
3. T
4. F
5. T
6. T
7. T
8. F
9. T
10. T
11. T
12. F

**Activity 11**

Answers will vary.

**Activity 12**

Answers will vary, but the following may serve as a guideline:

(Lines 11–15; 33–46) Glendower claims that the sky was filled with shooting stars and the earth quaked when he was born.

(Lines 16–18; 19–20; 22–32) Hotspur replies that the earth would have done the same if Glendower's cat had kittens—Hotspur is saying that it was a mere coincidence, if it happened at all.

(Line 50) Glendower claims that he can summon spirits.

(Lines 51 and 52) Hotspur claims that so can he, or anyone for that matter, but that does not mean that the spirits come when they are called.

(Line 53) Glendower claims that he can command Satan.

(Lines 54–58) Hotspur teases him by saying that by telling the truth, he can shame the devil (indicating that Glendower is lying about everything).

(Lines 116–121) Glendower says that he has transcribed English songs for the harp and even written music—something he says that Hotspur has never done.

(Lines 122–129) Hotspur says he would rather be a kitten than a cheap, cheesy, prissy poet.

### Activity 13

Answers may vary slightly.

1. He becomes angry and sends the messenger away empty-handed.
2. He rants and raves and is obsessed with antagonizing the King anyway that he can because the King has made him angry.
3. He is immediately supportive of this dangerous plan.
4. He makes fun of her and says that it is none of her business where he goes or what he does, but he does allow her to come with him.
5. He makes fun of them with coarse jokes to his wife.
6. He is courageous, a good soldier, a macho-man, sexist, hot-headed, and stubborn.

### Activity 14

Answers will vary.

### Activity 15

| | |
|---|---|
| 1. c | 7. h |
| 2. d | 8. e |
| 3. g | 9. b |
| 4. a | 10. f |
| 5. f | 11. h |
| 6. i | 12. a |

### Activity 16

Answers will vary.

### Activity 17

Answers will vary.

### Activity 18

Identifying quotations will vary.

Prince Henry: heir to the throne of England. He is known for his unprincely ways—namely thieving, carousing, and hanging around questionable people.

King Henry IV: overthrew last king, disappointed in his son, really wants to be liberating the holy lands from pagans instead of dealing with people like Northumberland, Worcester, and Hotspur, who want him deposed

Falstaff: loves women, wine, food, and steals for a living; is cowardly, loves Prince Hal, and tells tall tales constantly, especially about his own valor

Hotspur: son of Northumberland, hot-headed, valiant in battle, wants to overthrow King Henry, who he feels turned on him and his sister's husband (Mortimer) after being helped to the throne by them and others

Glendower: sorcerer who is antagonized by Hotspur—in on the plan to overthrow the King

Worcester: Hotspur's uncle who is the mastermind behind the plan to align with the armies of Scotland and York to overthrow King Henry

Mortimer: abandoned by the King, held prisoner now; married to a woman who only speaks Welsh; named heir to the throne by former king

Northumberland: Hotspur's father, one of the people planning to overthrow Henry

Poins: thief who plans to rob Falstaff and fellow thieves as a joke to see how cowardly they will turn out to be

Westmoreland: loyal earl to the King who told him of Mortimer's capture and his belief that Worcester put Hotspur up to refusing the King his prisoners

**Activity 19**

Answers will vary.

**Activity 20**

| | | | |
|---|---|---|---|
| 1. | b | 6. | c |
| 2. | c | 7. | d |
| 3. | d | 8. | b |
| 4. | e | 9. | a |
| 5. | f | 10. | d |

**Activity 21**

Answers may vary slightly.

1. Hotspur's father will not be coming to battle because he is ill.
2. Northumberland also will not be sending his army because he feels that no one but he can lead them—they won't rally around someone else.
3. Worcester is concerned that people will think Northumberland did not come to fight because their motives for this rebellion were not good enough. Thus, people will lose faith in them (the rebels).
4. Westmoreland and the Prince are marching toward them with 7,000 troops.
5. The King is also coming with his own large army.
6. Worcester cannot get his army together for two more weeks.

**Activity 22**

Answers will vary.

**Activity 23**

Answers will vary, but the following may serve as a guideline:

- King Henry unfairly taxed the entire state.
- He would not ransom Mortimer.
- He tried to trap Hotspur with spies and bring disgrace on Hotspur's battle victories.
- He banned Northumberland from court.
- He forgot the "little people" who helped him achieve the throne.
- He broke oaths he made before he was king and lied about it.

- He forced Hotspur and the rest to oppose him because he is now a tyrant.

**Activity 24**

Answers will vary.

**Activity 25**

Order of events:

Act one: 4, 2, 3, 1

Act two: 2, 4, 3, 1

Act three: 1, 4, 2, 3

Act four: 2, 1, 4, 3

**Activity 26**

Answers will vary.

**Activity 27**

Answers will vary, but the following may serve as a guideline:

Scene 1: Honor is fine to talk about, but it will not save your life or keep you safe. All the honor in the world will not prevent you from dying, so you have to look out for yourself, and do what you have to do.

Scene 3: He will be honorable if he must, but he does not care for the type of violent honor bestowed upon men who die on the battlefield; he would rather live.

Scene 4: Falstaff is claiming that he had discreet honor when he pretended to be dead because it saved his life. Obviously, most people would disagree.

**Activity 28**

Answers will vary.

**Activity 29**

Answers will vary.

**Activity 30**

1. F
2. F
3. T
4. F
5. T
6. F
7. F
8. F
9. T
10. F

**Final Test**

1. F
2. T
3. T
4. F
5. F
6. F
7. F
8. T
9. T
10. F
11. b
12. a
13. d
14. a
15. b
16. b
17. a
18. d
19. a
20. a

**Culminating Activity 1**

Presentations will vary, but the following may serve as a guideline for grading:

- Professional presentation style
- Stayed within time guidelines
- Gave each genre equal presentation time
- Did not misinterpret text
- Used text as support
- Insightful comments
- Followed guidelines of assignment

**Culminating Activity 2**

Essays will vary, but the following may serve as a guideline for grading:

- Strong thesis that remained the focus for entire paper

- Utilized textual support
- Stayed within length guidelines
- Properly attributed quotations from play
- Demonstrated understanding of text
- Thesis is well supported
- Used correct spelling and punctuation

**Culminating Activity 3**

Posters or book jackets will vary. Here are some possible grading guidelines:

- Colorful
- Easy to read
- Incorporates title
- Represents book and events appropriately

**Culminating Activity 4**

Plays will vary, but the following may serve as a grading guideline:

- Did not misinterpret events from play
- All group members participated in presentation
- Chose important events carefully and thoughtfully
- Enthusiastic performance; spoke loudly enough for everyone to hear
- Stayed within time guidelines

**Culminating Activity 5**

Responses will vary.

**Culminating Activity 6**

Responses will vary, but the following may serve as a grading guideline:

- Clear, professional, and energetic presentation style; spoke loudly enough for everyone to hear
- Stayed within time guidelines
- Gave each genre careful and equal consideration
- Did not misinterpret play
- Incorporated strong visual aid(s)